Para-Life
RESCUE!

Rob Waring, *Series Editor*

HEINLE
CENGAGE Learning™

Australia • Brazil • Japan • Korea • Mexico • Singapore • Spain • United Kingdom • United States

Words to Know

This story is set in South America. It takes place in and around the city of Rio de Janeiro [riːoʊ deɪ ʒəneəroʊ], Brazil.

BRAZIL

Rio de Janeiro

BRAZIL

SOUTH AMERICA

N W E S

 A **Beach Rescue!** Read the paragraph. Then match each word or phrase with the correct definition.

Most busy beaches around the world have lifeguards, particularly during the high season. It's a lifeguard's job to help when someone is having difficulty in the sea. They usually sit on the shore and use binoculars to see what is happening far out in the water. If someone seems to be drowning or having a problem swimming, they go into the sea to rescue the victim.

1. lifeguard _____

2. high season _____

3. binoculars _____

4. rescue _____

5. victim _____

a. save someone in danger

b. someone who suffers from an accident, crime, illness or bad luck

c. a person whose job is to save people from drowning

d. the time of year when a tourist area receives the most visitors

e. special glasses that make distant objects appear closer

A lifeguard and a paramotor pilot work together to help a victim.

 victim

B **Sky Rescue!** Read the paragraph. Then write the basic form of each underlined word next to the correct definition.

On the beaches of Rio de Janeiro, people are now combining paramotors with the work of lifeguards to save lives. Paramotors are a kind of paraglider that has a motor. The paramotor pilot fastens him- or herself into a lightweight frame that holds an engine. The propeller on the motor moves the paramotor through the air. Paramotor pilots have an aerial view of the beaches, so they can better see people in trouble. They can also easily manoeuvre their paramotors to reach victims quickly.

1. a piece of equipment that moves air or water by turning around quickly: _____
2. a structure which supports something: _____
3. taking place in the air: _____
4. an aircraft made of a large piece of material which a rider uses to sail on the wind: _____
5. turn and direct an object: _____
6. an aircraft which uses a large piece of material, a motor, and wind to move through the air: _____

paraglider

frame

lifeguard

paramotor

propeller

The Brazilian city of Rio de Janeiro – or 'Rio', as it is commonly known – is one of the most beautiful cities in the world. Its combination of impressive coastline with absolutely **stunning**[1] mountains attracts people from all over. Visitors often come to Rio on holiday, therefore its beaches are particularly crowded during high season. The region is sometimes very hot, and it is a favourite pastime to cool off in the sea.

Rio is also a city that offers more opportunities than just swimming and getting a suntan. Visitors and residents can also participate in a number of other activities – both on the sea and in the air. Sports like paragliding have long been very popular in this beautiful coastal region, and now there is a new type of glider in Rio; it is called the paramotor. The paramotor is a type of paraglider with a lightweight engine and a large propeller that is **strapped**[2] to the back of the pilot. The aircraft was originally invented for sports and **leisure**[3] use, but these days it is being used as a valuable search–and–rescue tool on and above Rio's beaches. In other words, paramotors are now saving lives.

---

[1]**stunning:** very beautiful
[2]**strap:** attach or hold, usually with a strong material
[3]**leisure:** free time

Skim for Gist

Read through the entire book quickly to answer the questions.

1. What is the book basically about?

2. Why are paramotors important to the story?

The use of paramotors for search–and–rescue actually began several years ago in a very remarkable way. Brazilian paragliding **champion**[4] and instructor **Ruy Marra**[5] was flying over the popular Copacabana Beach in Rio. He explains what happened: 'I was flying over Copacabana Beach in 1995, doing [an] advertisement for a company with [a] paramotor, when I saw a woman drowning under me,' he says. 'And then I was very worried. I [had] a **life preserver**[6] for myself, and then I had the idea to use [it] and to give [it to] her. So I put it on my leg, I came down, because it is easier to manoeuvre the paramotor. I [shouted to] her, and then I gave her the life preserver. That's the way it was with the first rescue in the world [with a] paramotor.'

---

[4]**champion:** the winner of a final contest
[5]**Ruy Marra:** [ruːi mɑːrɑː]
[6]**life preserver:** equipment, usually shaped as a ring, used to keep a person above water

It was a rescue that occurred entirely by accident, but it would have a lasting effect on Marra's life. Since that very first rescue in 1995, Marra has founded his own private business based upon the Para-Life Rescue System, which uses paramotors to rescue drowning people. He has developed this system into an important component of beach safety – not just in Rio, but all around Brazil. It's a business that has been very successful and has saved an amazing number of lives. Over the past few years, his staff of 20 people has been responsible for over 80 rescues. These days, Para-Life pilots are often cheered on by people on the crowded beaches as they take off and land. Everybody really likes to see them in the air because they know that they are safer in the water when the Para-Life pilots are nearby.

It wasn't easy for Marra to get started with his rescue system on the beaches of Rio. Initially, he was required to receive approval from the Brazilian government for his Para-Life business. Once that was obtained, he also had to get a cooperation agreement with the association of lifeguards who work on the beaches. It was important that they were willing to work with the Para-Life Rescue System to help people. But how did the lifeguards feel about the system? Did they feel that the Para-Life business was in competition with them, or did they feel it was a benefit?

In the end, the lifeguards turned out to be some of the biggest fans of the Para-Life pilots. Since both groups were in the business of saving lives, they decided to work together cooperatively. Lifeguards on the beach began to work with the Para-Life teams in the air by communicating through **two-way radios**.[7] This greatly **expanded**[8] the lifeguards' own search-and-rescue capabilities.

Since the two groups have started working together, saving people has definitely become a cooperative task. One of Rio's lifeguards explains that the paramotor pilots give them extra help in a few different ways. 'It is a great help to us,' he says, 'because it really helps to have an aerial view of the beach and the swimmers offshore. Once a person is sinking, the paramotor pilot can drop a life preserver to them and **sustain**[9] them until we get there.' It works out to be a perfect partnership.

---

[7]**two-way radio:** a kind of radio used for communication
[8]**expand:** grow larger or make bigger
[9]**sustain:** keep in existence by providing strength, support, or necessities

Before going into the sky to watch over the beaches, Para-Life pilots must prepare for their flight. First, they strap themselves into the lightweight but powerful frame that holds the propeller. The frame also holds a small **backpack**[10] equipped with a life preserver, binoculars and a two-way radio. In addition, the frame holds a small motor which turns the propeller and which can keep the aircraft in the air for up to three hours. Having the motor also allows the Para-Life pilot to get down to the water quite rapidly if necessary.

Once a victim is discovered in the sea, the pilot first calls in to the lifeguards, using the two-way radio. Then, the pilot flies against the wind to reduce flight speed and manoeuvres close enough to drop the life preserver to the swimmer who is having difficulties. The pilot then continues to fly above the victim until the lifeguards arrive, making sure that the victim is okay. It's an excellent example of land and air rescue services working together.

---

[10]**backpack:** a type of bag carried on the back with two shoulder straps and sometimes a metal frame

The beaches of Rio can get extremely crowded at certain times of the year, and the most people are on the beaches during the three-month-long high season in Rio de Janeiro. During this period, three Para-Life teams, with two pilots each, work Saturdays, Sundays and public holidays. They can only work as long as the winds are manageable; however, if it's too windy, it's not possible for them to be in the air.

In order to identify the highest-risk areas for swimmers, pilots often look for rip currents, which are responsible for most deaths by drowning. A rip current is a strong surface flow of water that's moving towards the sea from nearer to the shore. Such currents can be extremely dangerous as they often pull swimmers away from the beach. They can cause a person to drown after the swimmer becomes exhausted while attempting to fight the current. Rip currents may be very dangerous, but fortunately they are also easy for the Para-Life pilots to identify because they are lighter in colour than normal waves when seen from above. Once the Para-Life pilots know where the rip currents are, they can warn the lifeguards to ensure that people don't swim in the area.

Identify Cause and Effect

**Circle the cause and underline the effect
in each of the sentences.**

1. If it's too windy, it's not possible for the Para-
   Life pilots to be in the air.

2. In areas with rip currents, there are often
   increased numbers of drowning deaths.

3. Swimmers often drown when they become
   exhausted after trying to fight a rip current.

Not surprisingly, the Para-Life system is gaining in popularity. Marra's Para-Life system has received the interest of safety groups in many countries who would like to develop a safe, dependable rescue system, too. Soon, the Para-Life Rescue System could be used not only in Brazil, but also internationally. Marra now plans to start a Para-Life programme to teach people a combination of essential piloting skills and skills that are specific to water rescues. He also intends to offer a **paramedic**[11] course as well. All of Marra's courses will be certified, so the people who take them can become qualified paramotor pilots.

The pilots that are taking Marra's current training courses are able to manoeuvre their aircrafts with incredible skill. They can even race down the beach with their paramotors and catch life preservers with their feet! It's obvious that there is an increasing demand for pilots with this combination of skills. So what's in store for Marra's future?

---

[11] **paramedic:** a person trained to provide emergency medical help when a doctor is not present

In the future, Marra will still be saving people from drowning at the beach. However, he also has long-term plans and other goals and is not just thinking about the immediate future. If his plans go well, he'll also be teaching people everywhere how to use the Para-Life Rescue System. 'My long-term idea is to train people in other countries to [do] this,' he says, '[to train them] to use the Para-Life Rescue System and help the lifeguards, and push down the number of people drowning on the beach.'

Marra's plans mean that some day in the future, people on beaches everywhere may be able to look up into the sky and see a paramotor flying above them. These skilled pilots with their fast and manoeuvreable paramotors can make swimmers feel safer and more relaxed as they enjoy themselves. With the Para-Life Rescue System around, hopefully everyone's beaches will be safer someday soon!

After You Read

1. Some visitors come to Rio de Janeiro for the beautiful coastline.
   A. True
   B. False

2. The original purpose of the paramotor was to:
   A. save lives
   B. help fishermen
   C. enjoy flying
   D. search for boats

3. Which of the following is a good heading for page 7?
   A. Woman Rescues Man on Paramotor
   B. No Aid for Drowning Swimmer
   C. Marra Paraglides Over Copacabana
   D. Life Preserver Dropped from Paramotor

4. On page 8, why is the rescue described as 'entirely by accident'?
   A. because the paramotor crashed during it
   B. because there was a boat accident
   C. because Marra didn't plan for it to happen
   D. because the woman was drowning

5. Why was it hard for Marra to start Para-Life?
   A. He had to get permission from the government.
   B. He didn't have enough money to buy paramotors.
   C. He couldn't find a good team of workers.
   D. He couldn't get support from the Brazilian public.

6. The Para-Life team coordinate well _____ the Brazilian lifeguards.
   A. for
   B. with
   C. to
   D. by

7. What does the writer probably think about the lifeguards?
  A. They should make better use of the Para-Life team.
  B. They should provide financial support to Para-Life.
  C. They have successfully integrated Para-Life into their rescues.
  D. They need better equipment to communicate with.

8. Which of the following may prevent a paramotor from flying?
  A. heat
  B. currents
  C. crowds
  D. wind

9. In 'they often pull' on page 14, 'they' refers to:
  A. swimmers
  B. rip currents
  C. pilots
  D. lifeguards

10. What is the purpose of page 17?
  A. to talk about the short-term plans for Para-Life
  B. to congratulate Marra's success
  C. to explain how to get involved with Para-Life
  D. to praise the Para-Life team

11. Marra's plan is to have Para-Life teams _____ in other countries.
  A. drown
  B. survive
  C. operate
  D. ride

12. According to the writer, how does Para-Life make swimmers feel?
  A. daring
  B. adventurous
  C. fierce
  D. protected

Caught *in the* Current

by Peter Stevenson

It was my first visit to California. I had just completed my first year of university and I was ready for a real holiday. I stayed with my friend Gary and his family at their home at the beach in San Diego. One day, we were relaxing on the beach when Gary suddenly jumped up and said, 'Hey, Pete! Do you want to see how far out we can swim? The waves look wild out there!' 'Sure! Let's go,' I said, and we ran together into the water.

We entered the sea right next to a long dock that extended approximately 100 metres into the water. Later I would be informed it's never a good idea to swim beside a dock; they sometimes cause dangerous currents. We swam straight out from the shore and shouted to each other as we swam through the warm water. Then suddenly, I realised that Gary wasn't by my side anymore. I looked back toward the shore and he was about 20 metres behind me and disappearing fast. 'Gary, what's happening?' I shouted, but by that time he was too far away for me to hear.

San Diego Lifeguard Rescue Record			
Beach	**2005**	**2006**	**2007**
Rip Current Assists	23,990	32,753	33,490
High Wave Assists	6,127	7,103	7,574
River Assists	164	195	278
SCUBA Assists	159	217	160
Boating	**2005**	**2006**	**2007**
Boat Assists	2,425	4,610	4, 874
Passenger Assists	3,729	3,879	9,130

Suddenly, it became clear that I was in trouble. The water surrounding me was full of mud and I remembered that muddy water is a sign of a rip current, which can pull a swimmer out to sea. I began to swim back towards the beach, but the current kept pulling me further out. I became incredibly tired from fighting against it. I couldn't see Gary anywhere. Unexpectedly a giant wave pushed me beneath the water and held me there for what seemed like a lifetime. I could hardly breathe, but then suddenly I resurfaced!

At last, I heard a noise and looked into the sky where I saw a paramotor coming towards me. Soon a life preserver was dropped next to me. The pilot pointed to the left and shouted, 'Don't swim towards the shore! Swim along the coast to get out of the current.' After a few minutes, I made it out of the current and soon a lifeguard rescue boat helped me aboard, and there was Gary! We were both exhausted, but safe. I had always thought that paramotors were for fun, but now I know they can have a much greater purpose – saving lives!

Word Count: 390
Time: _____

Vocabulary List

aerial (3, 10)
backpack (13)
binoculars (2, 13)
champion (7)
expand (10)
frame (3, 13)
high season (2, 4, 14)
leisure (4)
life preserver (7, 10, 13, 17)
lifeguard (2, 3, 8, 10, 13, 14, 18)
manoeuvre (3, 7, 13, 17, 18)
paraglide (3, 4, 7)
paramedic (17)
paramotor (2, 3, 4, 5, 7, 8, 10, 17, 18)
propeller (3, 4, 13)
rescue (2, 3, 4, 7, 8, 10, 13, 17, 18)
strap (4, 13)
stunning (4)
sustain (10)
two-way radio (10, 13)
victim (2, 13)